What Do You Think?

Is Organic Food Better?

Andrew Langley

Heinemann Library
Chicago, Illinois

Customer Service 888-454-2279
Visit our website at
www.heinemannraintree.com

Editorial: Andrew Farrow and Rebecca Vickers
Design: Philippa Jenkins
Picture research: Melissa Allison and Ruth Blair
Production: Alison Parsons

Printed and bound in China

13 12 11 10 09
10 9 8 7 6 5 4 3 2 1

Library of Congress Cataloging-in-Publication Data
Langley, Andrew.
  Is organic food better? / Andrew Langley.
     p. cm.
  Includes bibliographical references and index.
  ISBN 978-1-4329-1670-1 (hc)
  1. Natural foods. I. Title.
  TX369.L36 2008
  641.5'636--dc22

                          2008014658

Acknowledgments
The publishers would like to thank the following for permission to reproduce photographs:
© Corbis pp. **10**, **38**, /David Ashley **9**, /Louise Gubb **27**, /Ludovic Maisant **14**; © FLPA pp. /Jim
Brandenburg/Minden Pictures **46**, /Nigel Cattlin **24**, **43**, /John Eveson **30**, /Foto Natura Stock **37**, /
Wayne Hutchinson **19**; © Getty Images pp. /Digital Vision **51**, /PhotoDisc **35**; /Stone **4**; © istockphoto
p. **29**; © Masterfile/Noel Hendrickson p. **20**; © PhotoEdit, Inc./David Young Wolff p. **7**; © Science
Photo Library pp. /Martin Bond **44**, /Robert Brook **41**, /Tony Craddock **19**, /Jim Gipe/AgstockUSA **17**,
/Philippe Psaila **23**, /Dave Reede/AgstockUSA **12**, /Thomas Schneider/AgstockUSA **13**, /Scott Sinklier/
AgstockUSA **36**, /Sinclair Stammers **33**; © Kate Shuster p. **49**.

Cover photograph: reproduced with permission of © Corbis/Steve Lupton.

Written source material on page 23 from the UK FSA is Crown copyright material reproduced with
permission of the Controller of HMSO and the Queen's Printer for Scotland.

Every effort has been made to contact copyright holders of any material reproduced in this book.
Any omissions will be rectified in subsequent printing if notice is given to the publishers.

The publishers would like to thank Padideh Sabeti for her assistance with the preparation of
this book.

Disclaimer
All the Internet addresses (URLs) given in this book were valid at the time of going to press.
However, due to the dynamic nature of the Internet, some addresses may have changed, or sites
may have changed or ceased to exist since publication. While the author and publishers regret any
inconvenience this may cause readers, no responsibility for any such changes can be accepted by
either the author or the publishers.

Table Of Contents

What Do You Think?...5

What Is Organic Food? 11

Is Organic Food Better For Us? 21

Is Organic Food Better For Animals?.................... 31

Is Organic Food Better For The Environment?.................. 39

Can We Change Anything?.................................... 45

Find Out More 52

Glossary 54

Index 56

Some words are printed in bold, **like this**. You can find out what they mean in the glossary on pages 54–55.

> *Chemical free*

Does an organically grown melon taste better than one grown with chemicals? Many people believe that organic food is healthier and tastier.

What Do You Think?

When you go into a store to buy apples, you must make a choice. There will be lots of different varieties on display, probably from several areas of the world as far apart as the United States, France, and New Zealand. So, how do you decide which variety to buy?

Then there is another big choice to make: Will you buy the ordinary apples or the ones marked "**organic**"? Do you even know what "organic" means? And what is the difference between an organic apple and an ordinary one? It may be more expensive, but does it taste better? Is it better for you?

The same choice applies to many kinds of food. Bread, meat, vegetables, breakfast cereal, fruit juice, even candy—there are organic versions of them all. Some people think that organic food is tastier and more healthy. They argue that farmers who use powerful chemicals to grow crops and animals are also harming the environment. Other people say that these chemicals allow farmers to produce more food than ever before. As Earth's population rises, this food will be desperately needed.

So, does it matter what kind of food we eat? Are some foods better than others? What are the real effects of "chemical" farming? Is organic food always safer? These issues touch everybody's life in some way. We must have the tools and the skills to join in the debate.

Your opinion counts

This series is called "What Do You Think?" This is a question aimed at you. You are involved, and your answer to the question matters. Maybe you do not have an opinion yet. But you are being asked to think about the subject. That means figuring out your own opinion and not just copying someone else. Having an opinion gives you the chance to tell other people your views. In thinking about this issue, you accept that it is worth debating and that it concerns you. The purpose of this book is to help you along the way and to guide you through the different aspects of the issue without trying to push you one way or the other.

✔ What do they think?

"From the beginning, my kids have eaten organic. . . The more I learn about food, the more amazed I am at how their properties can basically fix anything."
Gwyneth Paltrow, actress

"Tell me what you eat and I will tell you who you are."
Anthelme Brillat-Savarin, a French lawyer and writer (1755–1826)

Is there a right answer?

With a factual question, such as a math sum, there is only one correct answer. It is not something you can argue about. It is a matter of fact, not opinion. This book asks a different kind of question: "Is organic food better?" This is not a factual question, and there is no correct answer to it. People can debate the answer. It is a matter of opinion, not fact.

How do you form an opinion?

Everybody has opinions about all kinds of topics. Some people feel very strongly about organic food. But you need a lot more than strong feelings to reach an opinion that will stand up to debate. You need to look at the subject calmly and with an open mind.

The aim of this book is to help you to think for yourself about organic food. It shows you how to a form a balanced and well-informed opinion on the subject. To do this successfully, you need to follow a clear set of steps. You may be surprised at what you discover on the way.

> *Fresh from the farm*

Business is brisk at a farmer's market in California. Shoppers here can buy produce direct from the person who grows it. Is the quality of the food likely to be better than that of goods in a supermarket?

Why have an opinion?

Do you like to debate, or are you someone who keeps out of discussions? You may feel you have nothing to say or are not interested in the subject. Now is the time to change that. It is fun to discuss your opinions with others. It has other advantages, too. Debating your opinions with others:

* gets you involved with an issue
* gives you a broader view of the world
* encourages you to think logically
* gives you the chance to interact with other people
* helps you learn to stand up for yourself in a lively debate.

Can you change your opinion about food?

Are you interested in food? Is it an important part of your life? It ought to be, because a balanced diet is the foundation of healthy living. But many people know very little about what they put in their stomachs every day. If you want to take part in a debate about organic and non-organic food, you must think about what you eat. Here are some questions to ask:

• Where does my food come from?
• How was it produced?
• Is there anything in the food that might cause harm?
• How far has it traveled to reach me?
• Do I like eating it?

Three steps to making up your mind

As you read this book and think about organic food, approach the topic critically. Apply these three steps to each aspect of the topic:

Look

First, you need evidence. This is the raw material that gives you a firm base on which to build your opinion. Without facts you will not be able to back up an argument, no matter how passionately you believe in it. Evidence comes in many forms, including statistics, eyewitness accounts, public statements, and scientific reports.

Books and the Internet are good sources of evidence. Look in newspapers and magazines for up-to-date stories about the issue. Talk to people who know something about it. Don't forget that your own experience can also be useful. Has something happened in your life to make you think organic food is better than non-organic food?

Listen

There are two sides to any argument. Keep an open mind and listen carefully to the ideas and evidence of both sides—even when you disagree with them strongly. Above all, keep focused on the issue. A debate is often won by the person who is best at debating and has the strongest evidence. (You can read more about debating skills on pages 48–49.)

Think

When you read something or listen to someone, do you always believe what you are being told? Learn to be critical of what you read and hear. Do not just accept evidence and arguments at face value. This is the most important step of all. Take a hard look at the evidence and ask your own questions.

Is it fact, or just someone else's opinion? Is it from a reliable source? Is it **biased**—in other words, does the writer have a reason to favor one side of the argument or the other? Does he or she have an interest in trying to change your views?

> *Online information*
>
> **You need evidence to help you form a worthwhile opinion. The Internet is a good place to start looking.**

> *Hoeing weeds*

A farmer weeds his strawberry field the old-fashioned organic way, with a tractor-drawn hoe. Many growers now use chemical sprays to get rid of weeds.

What Is Organic Food?

Food is the fuel that keeps our bodies going. But is there more to it? Good food is also one of life's pleasures. Cooking and eating it plays a big part in our daily lives. Growing food is probably the single most important industry in the world, even today.

For most of human history, farmers grew crops and raised animals in a simple way. There were no artificial chemicals to kill weeds or make plants grow faster. There were no factories to process food or put it in cans. People ate food that was mostly fresh and local. Today, we would call it organic.

But our food has changed dramatically over the past 50 years. For a start, we can produce a lot more of it. Modern chemicals and machines allow farmers to produce far bigger crops of grains and other plants, as well as much more meat, milk, and other foods. Many people eat food that has been processed and packaged. Our food also travels farther to reach us, even from the other side of the world. The vast majority of our food today is non-organic.

Do you know what the term "organic" means? You might think it means rejecting chemicals and growing things "naturally." But organic food and organic farming involve a lot more than that. Before you can form an opinion on the topic, you must know what you are talking about.

Organic food: What does it mean?

The word "organic" strictly means "to do with living things." How does that relate to our food? A hamburger is made with meat from a cow, which was a living thing. So, are all hamburgers organic? No. In order to be called organic, food has to have been produced in a certain way, according to guidelines. The definition of organic food differs slightly around the world.

This is the definition from the U.S. Department of Agriculture (USDA):

What Is Organic?

Organic food is produced by farmers who emphasize the use of renewable resources and the conservation of soil and water to enhance environmental quality for future generations. Organic meat, poultry, eggs, and dairy products come from animals that are given no **antibiotics** or **growth hormones**. Organic food is produced without using most conventional **pesticides**; petroleum-based **fertilizers** or sewage sludge-based fertilizers; bio-engineering; or ionizing radiation. Before a product can be labeled "organic," a Government-approved certifier inspects the farm where the food is grown to make sure the farmer is following all the rules necessary to meet USDA organic standards. Companies that handle or process organic food before it gets to your local supermarket or restaurant must be certified, too.

[Source: www.ams.usda.gov/nop]

> Chemicals from the air

Many modern crop fields are so big, it is easiest to spray them from an aircraft. This one is covering plants with **fungicide**, to kill potential diseases.

> *Natural goodness*

Animal **manure** is spread onto a field before a new crop is sown. This puts **nutrients** back into the soil.

✔ Four organic principles

One worldwide organization promotes organic food and farming: the International Federation of Organic Agriculture Movements (IFOAM). These are IFOAM's four principles:

✓ Organic farming must sustain and improve the health of the soil, plants, animals, humans, and the planet.

✓ Organic farming should be based on living ecological systems and cycles. It must work with them, learn from them, and help to protect them.

✓ Organic farmers should build up relationships that give fair treatment to our common environment and our opportunities in life.

✓ Organic farms should be managed in a careful and responsible way, so that they protect the health and well-being of people both now and in the future.

[Source: Adapted extract from the IFOAM website, www.ifoam.org]

What's new about organic food?

In simple terms, nothing is new about organic food. It has been around as long as humans. Our earliest ancestors were hunters and gatherers who ate wild animals and plants. All their food was organic, from berries and nuts to deer and rabbits. It grew in completely natural conditions.

The first farmers raised their crops and animals without artificial chemicals or medicines. They used natural fertilizers to enrich the soil. For example, Chinese peasants spread their own sewage on the rice fields. Native Americans living on the coast buried fish near their maize (corn) plants to fertilize them.

How did traditional farming work?

For many centuries, most farmers grew food in this natural way. They fed their cattle and sheep on grass, hay, and vegetables. Pigs roamed the woods, eating nuts and roots. Farmers used the manure from these animals to fertilize the soil for crops. They pulled up weeds by hand. They attacked pests and plant diseases with simple mixtures made from sulfur or tobacco leaves.

Some things changed, of course. New machines were invented, such as plows for turning the soil and drills for sowing seeds. After the 18th century, people developed more efficient ways of using land and feeding **livestock**. Farmers also learned how to breed bigger and better cattle, sheep, and pigs. Despite these developments, most food remained strictly organic.

Are the old ways still used today?

In some parts of the world, such as Africa and Asia, farming has changed little since ancient times. Here is a report of one example. On Java, an island in Indonesia, villagers have used their own organic farming methods for over 1,000 years.

> The old ways

The kind of farming seen in this rice paddy field in Southeast Asia has changed very little for many centuries.

Village Agroforests In Java

In their small plots, Javanese peasants mix a large number of different plant species. Within one village, up to 250 different species may be grown: annual herbs, **perennial** herbaceous plants, climbing vines, creeping plants, shrubs, and trees. Livestock form an important component of this **agroforestry** system—particularly poultry, but also sheep grazing freely or fenced in sheds and fed with **forage** gathered from the vegetation. Fishponds are also common and the fish are fed with animal and human wastes [excrement].

Natural processes of cycling water and organic matter are maintained. Dead leaves and twigs are left to decompose, keeping a continual litter layer and humus through which nutrients are recycled. Compost, fishpond mud, and green manures are used on cropland. These forms of recycling maintain soil fertility without the use of chemical fertilizers.

[Source: The United Nations FAO website, www.fao.org]

Would this kind of farming feed many people? Is it an efficient or a wasteful way to grow food? Would Javanese peasants eat better if they used chemical fertilizers in their agroforests? Would that cost them more?

✔ A mixed farm

Two hundred years ago, most farms in North America and Europe were mixed. Farmers did not specialize in one product, but rather grew a mixture of different animals and crops. Here are some of the animals and crops found on mixed farms:

Livestock		Crops	
chickens	sheep	wheat	maize (corn)
ducks	goats	vegetables	fruits
geese	cattle	hay	
horses	pigs		

How many of these crops and animals do you see on modern farms today?

Why did farming have to change?

Traditional organic farming methods encountered two big problems. The first was disease. Throughout history, farming suffered from all kinds of pests. **Microbes**, insects, and **parasites** destroyed whole crops and killed huge numbers of animals. Sometimes this caused widespread famine. Some of the diseases, such as anthrax and tuberculosis (TB), affected humans as well.

The second problem was the growing population. The number of people in the world began to grow with amazing speed. Between 1825 and 1927 the population doubled. Today, there are six times more hungry mouths to feed than there were in 1825. Farmers needed to find ways to grow much more food on their land.

✔ Population landmarks

Around 10,000 years ago there were an estimated 10 million (0.01 billion) people in the world. This is how the total has since risen:

Population landmark	Year reached	Time taken
0.5 billion	1500	
1 billion	1825	2 million years
2 billion	1927	102 years
3 billion	1960	33 years
4 billion	1975	15 years
5 billion	1986	11 years
6 billion	2000	14 years

In 2007 the world's population was estimated to be over 6.6 billion.

[Adapted from: Colin Tudge, *So Shall We Reap*, London: Allen Lane (2003).]

The coming of chemicals

During the first half of the 20th century, scientists developed a range of new fertilizers, pesticides, and **herbicides**. These artificial products could be made in vast quantities in chemical factories.

The most important of these new chemicals was nitrate fertilizer. **Nitrogen** is a very important element in the growth of plants—the more you give plants, the bigger they grow. In the 1920s, scientists found a simple way to make artificial nitrate fertilizer. This transformed farming around the world. Today, farmers spread almost 100 million tons of nitrates (most of it made from natural gas) on the soil every year.

The Green Revolution

The new chemicals were part of an agricultural revolution. Improved seeds and better feeds for livestock were also developed, as well as new machinery. Together these innovations had a drastic effect on the world's food production. In some areas, between 1961 and 2000 the harvests of wheat doubled in size. In Asia, they increased by five times.

The production of meat, rice, fruits, vegetables, and other foods also rose dramatically during this period. It became known as the Green Revolution, and probably prevented widespread famine in the developing world.

Wheat production (millions of tons)	1961	2000
Africa	5.6	15.3
Asia	50.3	254
Australia	7.4	24.5
Europe	36.5	110
North & Central America	47	101

[Source: The United Nations FAO website, www.fao.org]

> *Monster machines*

A fleet of giant combine harvesters moves through a wheat field. They cut the wheat and separate the grain from the stalks.

What do they think?

"I do try to feed my children as much as possible on organic food but find it quite expensive. My brother goes to the extreme where he buys organic clothes and diapers. I think it can only be good for you and better than having lots of chemicals pumped into your body."

A contributor to an online discussion forum

What's the difference?

Today, the vast majority of our food is produced using some chemical products. Plants are grown in soil fertilized with nitrates and sprayed with pesticides and weed killers. Animals are raised on food grown in the same way. They are also treated with chemical medicines and **vaccines**. None of this food can be called organic.

To be organic, farmers cannot use any of these artificial products on the soil, crops, or animals. They can only use natural fertilizers, such as manure (animal droppings) or ground minerals, and pesticides made from natural materials.

How different are the lives of organic and non-organic cows? Read the extracts below. Remember to think critically. Where do these articles come from?

The Life of a Dairy Cow on a Modern Non-Organic Farm

Dairy cows always have access to feed and fresh, clean water.

Farmers ensure that their cows have room to lie down, stretch, eat, and drink comfortably.

Many dairy farmers have installed rubber or other non-slip flooring in their barns to make it easier for the cows to move around. Cows may sleep on waterbeds, sand beds, or mattresses made of rubber, foam, or a combination of the two.

Most dairy barns use advanced ventilation systems to assure healthy air quality. On warm days, farmers use fans and misting devices to keep cows cool and comfortable.

Farmers employ professional nutritionists to develop a scientifically formulated, balanced, and nutritious diet for their cows. Diets include hay, grains, **protein** sources (such as soy), and other vitamins and minerals.

Cows receive regular veterinary care, including periodic check-ups, preventative vaccinations, and prompt treatment of illness.

[Source: The Best Food Nation website run by U.S. food councils and associations, www.bestfoodnation.com]

> *Milking time*

These black and white Holsteins are in a modern milking unit. These cows have been bred to give huge amounts of milk.

The Life of a Dairy Cow on a Modern Organic Farm

Organic Milk Co-operative cows roam and graze in lush meadows for as much of the year as possible. They enjoy a natural diet of forage such as grass, hay, clover, **silage**, and cereals.

During the winter when the cows are not grazing pastures, they have plenty of space and comfortable bedding in well aired barns.

Homeopathic and herbal medicines are used to keep organic cows healthy and to treat ailments. Organic farmers use antibiotics only when the cow is actually ill, never just as a routine preventative treatment. They may also be used to alleviate suffering.

[Source: The Organic Milk Co-operative website]

> *Cows in clover*

Dairy cows graze in the natural environment of a rich alpine meadow in Bavaria, Germany.

> *Organic or not?*

When you go shopping for food, do you look specifically for organic produce?

Is Organic Food Better For Us?

Many people argue that the only aim of farming should be to grow enough food to feed the world. They believe farmers can only do this by using large amounts of chemicals— fertilizers and pesticides on plants, and growth boosters and other medicines on animals. This is the case even though farmers in some parts of the world produce too much food, and the surplus has to be destroyed. Without these chemicals, crops and livestock would grow more slowly and be more prone to disease.

Other people say that these chemicals are dangerous to humans. Scientists have found traces of pesticides in fruits and vegetables. Fumes from agricultural sprays can pollute the air. Nitrates from fertilizer get into our drinking water. All this poses a big risk to our health, they say.

Supporters of organic food argue that it is much safer to eat than non-organic produce. Organically grown plants do not contain chemical residues. Milk, meat, and eggs from organic animals are also more healthy. Moreover, they taste much better.

But how real is the danger from chemicals? Can traces of pesticide in a vegetable really threaten our health? Is there any evidence that organic food is actually better for us? Is it more nutritious? Does it really taste better?

Organic food: The healthy option?

There are two ways to look at any argument—the positive way and the negative way. The positive approach looks at reasons for eating organic food. The negative approach looks at the reasons not to eat conventional (non-organic) food. Starting with the positive approach, is organic produce better for you? Look at this news story:

Another Benefit Is Seen in Buying Organic Produce

A new study finds that organically grown tomatoes have higher levels of **flavonoids,** which may protect against cardiovascular [heart] disease. Researchers said the level of one flavonoid in the organic tomatoes was almost twice as high as that in conventionally grown tomatoes. Because of evidence that flavonoids may fight age-related diseases, researchers have been trying to develop crops with higher levels of them.

The researchers, from the University of California, Davis, looked at tomatoes grown over a 10-year period in organic fields and regular ones. The lead author of the study, Alyson E. Mitchell, said she was surprised at the extent of the difference. "We sort of went into this expecting higher levels" Dr. Mitchell said. "We did not expect to find the levels that we found."

[By Eric Nagourney, *New York Times*, July 17, 2007.]

What can you learn from this story? First, organic tomatoes have higher levels of flavonoids than non-organic ones. Second, flavonoids "may" help people to fight certain diseases connected with aging. But can you trust this report? Do you think the researchers were completely open-minded when they conducted their research?

Here are some other news stories from the same period:

"U.S. researchers discovered that organically grown kiwi fruits had much higher levels of vitamin C and polyphenols than conventional ones. These compounds are thought to help in reducing **cholesterol,** improving circulation, and preventing cancer."

[Source: *Daily Telegraph*, March 2007.]

"European researchers discover that mothers consuming mostly organic milk and meat products have about 50 percent more rumenic acid in their breast milk. Rumenic acid is responsible for most of the health benefits of milk and meat."

[Source: *British Journal of Nutrition*, July 2007.]

What do all these stories have in common? Do they make good evidence?

> *Increasing the crop*

Scientists are working all the time to find ways to grow more and bigger food products. Here, a researcher is Spain measures the size of a tomato.

Do all scientists support organic food?

Not everybody agrees that there is anything special about organic food. Here is part of a speech given by John Krebs, head of the Food Standards Agency in the United Kingdom, in 2003:

"In our view the current scientific evidence does not show that organic food is any safer or more nutritious than conventionally produced food. Nor are we alone in this assessment. For instance, the French Food Safety Agency (AFSSA) has recently published a comprehensive 128-page review which concludes that there is no difference in terms of food safety and nutrition. Also, the Swedish National Food Administration's recent research report finds no nutritional benefits of organic food."

✔ What do they think?

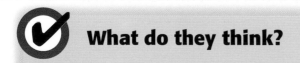

"I think organic food producers are just taking advantage of people's ignorance toward science nowadays."
A contributor to an online discussion forum

Are chemicals in non-organic food harming us?

Looking at the negative side of the argument, is non-organic food actually bad for us? Are the artificial fertilizers, pesticides, and herbicides used by conventional farmers dangerous to our health?

Most scientific surveys admit that small amounts (residues) of these chemicals find their way into some of the food we eat. Fruits and vegetables are the most likely to be contaminated. Many scientists say that very small amounts of chemicals are not harmful. Most national governments set limits for the maximum level of residues permitted in food. However, some scientists believe that these are poisonous substances and should not be allowed in food at all.

✔ Chemicals in our food

In the U.S. Department of Agriculture Pesticide Data Program Report of 2006, 60 different types of food were tested:

✓ 30 percent contained no detectable pesticide residues.

✓ 30 percent contained residues of one kind of pesticide.

✓ 40 percent contained residues of more than one kind of pesticide.

> Is this food safe to eat?

Many governments now have food tested to measure the amount of chemical residue.

How dangerous are pesticides?

Of course pesticides are poisonous. That's their job. They are meant to kill things—insects, fungi, and plant diseases. Tiny amounts in our food may not do us much harm, according to some scientists. But what about the people who use these chemicals or live near the fields they are sprayed on? Are they at greater risk?

What about the sprays and fertilizers used by organic farmers? Are they completely safe? Several substances used to make "organic" pesticides are poisonous to humans. These include derris (made from plant roots), nicotine (made from tobacco leaves), and pyrethrum (made from dried flower heads).

✔ Pesticide poisoning

✓ Every year 1–5 million people suffer pesticide poisoning around the world.

✓ More than 18,000 of these people die.

✓ Poisoning occurs through eating, drinking, or breathing polluted air.

✓ Children and expectant mothers face a higher risk.

✓ 99 percent of pesticide deaths happen in developing countries, though they use only 25 percent of the world's production of pesticides.

[Source: The 2004 Joint Report by the World Health Organization (WHO), Food and Agriculture Organization (FAO), and the United Nations Environmental Program (UNEP)]

Is non-organic food less nutritious?

In addition to the possible effects of chemical residues in non-organic food, we should consider whether food grown this way contains as many healthy nutrients as food grown organically.

"A scientific study shows that the nutrient content of conventionally grown fruits and vegetables has dropped markedly since the 1950s.

"The study comes from the University of Texas, where biochemist Donald R. Davis decided to try to quantify anecdotal reports of a trade-off between crop yields and concentrations of nutrients. He compared historic and current U.S. Department of Agriculture data on 43 garden crops (vegetables, strawberries, and melons) and found that the modern produce had lost protein (down an average of 6%), calcium (down 16%), vitamin C (down 20%), riboflavin (down 38%) and phosphorus (down 9%).

"What does this mean? According to the study, it may mean that methods that boost crop yields, such as chemical fertilization, irrigation, and **genetic breeding**, decrease the amount of some nutrients in the crop. The theory is that when plants are made to grow bigger and faster, they are not able to draw as many nutrients from the sun or soil. So those tangerine-sized strawberries may be as devoid of nutrition as they are of taste."
[Source: *LA Times*, March 2006.]

Feeding the world

Modern farming is all about growing as much food as possible. Scientific advances have led to a three-time increase in the output of the world's farms over the past 60 years. But have these advances solved the problem of world hunger? The answer is no. In some developing areas, notably Africa, food supplies have fallen catastrophically in recent years. Famine still kills many thousands of people every year.

Famine—natural or human-made?
Is this always the fault of bad or inefficient farming? Famine is often caused by other factors, such as drought and floods, civil war, and corrupt governments. All the same, farming practices do have a large part to play. Even the United States has its problems, as this piece shows:

Lowest Food Supplies in 50 or 100 Years: Global Food Crisis Emerging

Today, the United States Department of Agriculture (USDA) released its first projections of world grain supply and demand for the coming crop year: 2007/08. "USDA predicts global grain supplies will drop to their lowest levels on record. Further, it is likely that, outside of wartime, global grain supplies have not been this low in a century, perhaps longer," said NFU Director of Research Darrin Qualman. Most important, 2007/08 will mark the seventh year out of the past eight in which global grain production has fallen short of demand. In addition to falling grain supplies, global fisheries are faltering.

Demand for food is rising rapidly. There is a worldwide push to proliferate a North American style meat-based diet based on intensive livestock production—turning feed grains into meat. Qualman cautioned that there are no easy fixes. "If we try to do more of the same, if we try to produce, consume, and export more food while using more fertilizer, water, and chemicals, we will only intensify our problems."

[Source: A report by the National Farmers Union of Canada, May 11, 2007]

A future food shortage?

The world's population is growing fast. Can organic farming methods produce enough food for everyone? Trials in the United States have grown organic and non-organic crops side by side. Most of these show that organic methods can produce just as much food.

> *Feeding the hungry*

Food aid is distributed in a country hit by famine. Can organic farmers grow enough to feed everyone in the world?

Does organic food taste better?

Everybody has their own ideas about what tastes good. So, it is difficult to make a general statement about whether one kind of food tastes better than another. However, organic food growers often claim that their products have more flavor than non-organic. How can we decide if they are right? Look at these four pieces of evidence.

"A recent consumer poll has revealed that taste is a significant factor in people's choice to go organic— with over 90 percent saying that enjoying a tastier diet is an important motivation. Fruits and vegetable score particularly highly on taste with 72 percent saying they taste better than non-organic. Meat also scores highly with 71 percent saying they prefer the taste of organic."

[Source: The website of the Soil Association]

"The study found that organic orange juice was perceived as tasting better than conventional orange juice; however, no differences were found between organic and conventional milk. Therefore, it is concluded that the global claim that 'organic food tastes better' is not valid, and each product should be treated separately before a claim can be made."

[By Laurence Fillion and Stacey Arazi, *Nutrition and Food Science Journal*, 2002.]

"Some people who favor organic foods claim that they taste better. However, there is so much flavor variation among different varieties, different degrees of ripeness or freshness, or length of storage of the same fruit or vegetable, that it is very difficult for individuals to make true comparisons. Generally, when attempts have been made to carry out scientifically designed blind-tasting tests on the same variety, organic versus non-organic, taste panels have been unable to detect a flavor difference."

[Source: Institute of Food Science and Technology]

"Animals apparently have a much better sense of taste than humans do. In food-testing experiments, when animals were given a choice between organic and conventionally grown food, they significantly chose organic."

[Source: *Ecological Agriculture*, The Royal Danish Veterinary and Agricultural University, May 23, 2002.]

Do these articles change your opinion? Note that three of them are from scientific sources, while the first one is from an environmental group that campaigns for organic farming. Should this make a difference in the way you assess the evidence?

✔ Why do people go organic?

A 2005 survey of 1,000 Americans found that they eat organic food:

✓ to avoid pesticides (70.3%)

✓ for health and nutrition (67.1%)

✓ for freshness (68.3%)

✓ to avoid genetically modified foods (55%)

✓ for a better environment (52.4%).

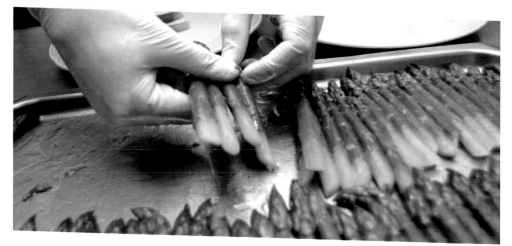

> Cooking organic
A chef prepares asparagus in a restaurant kitchen. Are people happy to pay higher prices for organic meals?

✔ What do they think?

"The first time I ate organic wholegrain bread I swear it tasted like roofing material." *Robin Williams, actor*

"The difference is amazing. The organic tomato has a natural lusciousness, it's succulent, it's juicy, and it's sweeter." *Marilyn Joyce, writer*

"Instead of popping pills we should eat more organic food." *Antony Worrall Thompson, chef*

> *The great outdoors*

Are chickens who live and feed
outdoors healthier and happier?

Is Organic Food Better For Animals?

Where does our food come from? How is it grown? These are questions that should be important to us because the food we eat controls our health. But we must not forget that it also affects many millions of other animals. Vast numbers of pigs, cattle, poultry, and other animals are killed every day so that we can eat meat. Herds of dairy cows give us milk, and chicken flocks give us eggs. Most of these farm animals are raised in non-organic ways. They eat food that was grown using chemicals. Many are dosed with medicines to prevent illnesses and with artificial growth promoters to make them produce more meat more quickly. How do these things affect their health and the quality of their lives?

Another feature of modern farming is the "intensive" method of raising animals. This is aimed at producing food as quickly and cheaply as possible. On many **intensive farms**, cattle, poultry, and pigs are kept indoors for much of their lives. Some live in crowded sheds or even in cages. Does this make them less happy or healthy?

Organic farmers in most countries try to raise their livestock in more natural conditions. Animals live mainly outdoors. They are fed on naturally grown foods and are only given medication when necessary to treat disease. But does this make them any happier?

The life of a dairy cow

Do you drink milk or eat cheese, butter, or yogurt? Dairy farming is one of the biggest—and most complicated—parts of the farming industry. But do you know what dairy farming involves?

Do dairy cows chew grass in open fields most of the time, then wander in to be milked? Governments have encouraged dairy farmers to increase their production of milk and meat massively. The result, in many places, is a highly intensive system. Here is part of a fact sheet issued by the U.S. Animal Protection Institute:

Get the Facts: The Destructive Dairy Industry

The dairy farms of today are quite different than the picturesque sunshine-filled meadows of contented cows we imagined as children. Today, most dairy cattle are confined to a barren fenced lot with a packed dirt floor, where they must endure all types of weather, including rain and extreme temperatures 24 hours a day.

To boost their milk production, the cattle are fed high intensity feeds and grains that often cause digestive upset. They are also injected with Bovine Growth Hormone (BGH) to increase by up to 25 percent the already exorbitant amount of milk they produce. Of the 9 million dairy cattle in the U.S., 7–25 percent are injected with BGH.

Up to 33 percent of dairy cows develop mastitis, a very painful udder infection that can become **systemic**, and is a common reason for early slaughtering. Abnormally large udders produce problems walking, so a cow's legs are usually spread apart, distorting the normal configurations of her pelvis and spine. Her back problems are aggravated when she must walk on hard ground and concrete.

Think critically about this evidence. Is the source reliable? Does the writer give a balanced or a biased picture of dairy farming? What definite facts can you gather? Do any of the problems described here apply equally to organic farming methods?

What does a dairy cow eat?
Cattle kept in dairy sheds rarely eat fresh grass. In 2001 over 75 percent of U.S. dairy cattle had no access to pasture land. Instead they are given "high intensity" feeds made of cereal, soybeans, and other starchy foods. These provide energy for the cow to produce a lot of milk, but they also cause upset stomachs. Cows have a complicated digestive system. It is perfectly adapted

to digesting grass, but not so good at digesting grains. Starchy diets increase the amount of acid in a cow's stomach. This can lead to all kinds of problems, including lameness and infected milk.

✔ The milk machine

How much milk does a cow produce in a year? This table shows how the average milk yield for an individual cow in the United States has risen since the 1960s. A big reason for this rise has been the use of growth hormones and more **concentrated** feeds.

Year	1965	1970	1975	1980	1985	1990	1995	2000	2004
Pounds	7,865	9,543	10,142	11,627	12,758	14,782	16,405	18,197	18,957

[Source: USDA National Agriculture Statistics Service, http://nass.usda.gov/Charts_and_Maps_Production_ and_Milk_Cows]

> *The tragedy of "mad cows"*

BSE (or "mad cow" disease) struck Great Britain in 1985. It was caused by mixing material from infected sheep into cattle feed. Thousands of cattle had to be killed and burned.

What makes a cow happy?

We have seen how the intensive, non-organic farming of dairy cattle produces vast amounts of milk, but it can also lead to disease and other physical problems. Do these intensive methods actually cause distress to the cows?

What do cows need to live a normal and contented life? First, they need food—and it has to be the right kind of food, which they can digest properly. Second, cows are sociable animals. They are used to being part of a herd, and they need to be able to hear, see, and touch other cows.

Is the organic way better?

Are dairy cows happier on organic farms? Once again, it is hard to give a definite answer. Different countries have different rules about what qualifies as organic farming. Some allow farmers to keep their cattle indoors and feed them on concentrate. This makes them much the same as the intensive, non-organic systems.

A tale of two cows

	Conventionally reared cow	Organically reared cow
Name	An ID number	Daisy, Peaches, etc.
Average Life	4–5 years	10+ years
Average daily milk output	54 pounds	43+ pounds*
Primary diet	Silage, hay, and commercial feed that can include corn, barley, fishmeal, potato waste	Grass from pastureland and hay, with some organic feed
Additives/ medicine	Bio-engineered growth hormones, antibiotics	Occasional vitamins and herbs
Living quarters	Dairy "feed lots" or barns, sometimes in stalls where they are machine milked	Spacious barns or stalls, lots of outdoor time
Breeding	Artificial insemination	Mating with bulls

* Organic output can be 20 percent less, in part because farmers often push the animals less hard.

[Source: The U.S. Department of Agriculture]

Other countries insist that organic dairy cows must be allowed to graze in the open air. In March 2005 organic farmers in the United States started a campaign to change the rules on organic milk, so that organic cows had to be able to graze on pastureland for most of the year. They won their battle.

How different is an organic dairy farm?
Many organic dairy farms claim to give their cows a more natural life. The animals spend most of the year outside eating grass. In the winter they live in airy sheds, supplied with grass-based food, such as hay and silage. They are given plenty of space to move around and are kept in their social groups.

What about chemicals? The cows are generally treated with herbal and homeopathic medicines. If they get seriously sick or are in pain, they are given antibiotics. Their winter feed usually includes cereals and soybeans, but these must be organically grown.

> *The milk supply*

Dairy cows will only give milk when they have a new calf. The calf is taken away after a short period so that the mother's milk can be supplied to humans instead.

What about other animals?

Many other kinds of animals are raised on farms, such as beef cattle, sheep, chickens, and pigs. How are they treated on conventional farms?

Chickens

Most of the chicken meat in the stores comes from animals that have spent their short lives in huge sheds. Tens of thousands are crammed together in **broiler houses**. They have little room to move and are kept in dim light so they stay calm. Most egg-laying hens have an even worse time. They are housed in wire cages ("batteries"), on mesh floors that slope so that the eggs roll out for easy collection.

> *Poultry prison*

Chickens are crammed together in a huge broiler shed. They have no room to move around and no natural light.

Pigs

Pigs are highly intelligent animals. But on intensive farms they, too, are crowded together in large, dimly lit sheds. In many countries, sows are confined in narrow stalls where they can lie down, but cannot turn around. The piglets have to crawl under an iron bar to suck their mother's milk.

Sheep

Sheep probably lead the most natural lives of all farm animals—organic or non-organic. The vast majority live outdoors, feeding on grass, hay, and pelleted food in winter.

The crowded conditions of intensive farming can cause diseases to spread very rapidly, so poultry and pigs are frequently dosed with antibiotics and other medicines. The animals suffer from high levels of stress and boredom (which leads chickens, for example, to peck each other).

Is the organic way kinder?

An "organic" label on food may simply mean that the animals were fed on organically grown food. It may not guarantee that they were raised naturally and humanely.

There is no worldwide definition of what "organic farming" means. In fact, many farmers do not know whether they are technically organic or not.

In much of the developing world, farms are still run in the old traditional way, using no chemicals. The animals live in natural conditions, eating grass or other wild plants. They are not treated with growth promoters or antibiotics. This sort of farming is certainly organic. But are the animals better off? Are they treated cruelly at times? When they get sick or injured, are they given medicine or painkillers? Are humane methods used to slaughter pigs, chickens, or cattle? An organic farmer is not necessarily a caring farmer, any more than a non-organic farmer is necessarily a cruel one.

> A free-range life

A rooster crows in an outdoor yard. Free range poultry lead a more natural life than indoor birds. They can scratch the soil to find a more varied diet.

> *Flowery fields*

Poppies flourish in this organic Californian mountain meadow. If the field were regularly sprayed with chemicals, there would be no flowers.

Is Organic Food Better For The Environment?

What does the word "food" make you think of? Eating it? Cooking it? Unwrapping a chocolate bar? Our idea of food is generally focused on ourselves—our stomachs and our taste buds. We have seen how our food also has a crucial link with farm animals and their welfare.

But the subject of food has far wider implications. Farming—the production of food—has a massive effect on the world around us. Since farming began we have cut down woodland, plowed up grassland, and grazed herds of animals. Even today, huge areas of the Amazon rainforest are being cleared to make way for crops and cattle.

The future of the planet depends largely on the way we treat the land. So, are non-organic farming methods severely harming the environment? Many people think they are. They say that chemical pesticides are damaging wildlife, and nitrates are polluting rivers and lakes.

Are organic farming methods any better? If we stopped using chemicals, would the damage stop, too? Organic farmers say they are doing much more than simply using natural fertilizers and pest controls. They are actively caring for the land and trying to grow our food in a way that can be sustained for centuries to come.

Fertilizers and global warming

Many farmers throughout the world depend on nitrogen fertilizers to make their crops grow well. Since the 1960s, they have been using it in ever bigger quantities. What is this wonder substance made of? The answer is **fossil fuels**. Every year, millions of tons of mineral oil and natural gas are processed to make nitrogen fertilizer.

This releases **carbon dioxide** into the atmosphere, just as cars and aircraft do. Studies have shown that the use of nitrates in farming generates 275 million tons of carbon dioxide emissions every year. This gas is one of the major contributors to global warming

What has happened to our water?

Nitrogen fertilizers, along with waste liquids from intensive livestock farms, do not just stay in the ground. They are washed out by the rain and drain into streams, ponds, and rivers. This causes water plant life to grow too fast, which in turn ruins a waterway's **ecosystem**. This can be a catastrophe for fish and other kinds of animal life. High levels of nitrates in water are not good for humans either, as these reports show:

"Nitrate in drinking water can cause methemoglobinemia, a potentially fatal condition in infants commonly known as blue-baby syndrome."
[Source: Environmental Working Group]

"The growing premature birth rate in the United States appears to be strongly associated with increased use of pesticides and nitrates."
[Source: *Science Daily*, May 2007.]

"There [is] a significant relationship between the levels of nitrate in drinking water and risk of death from bladder cancer."
[Source: *Journal of Toxicology*, January 2007.]

"The National Cancer Institute suggests a link between elevated levels of nitrate in drinking water and an increased risk of cancer of the lymphatic system."
[Source: Minnesota Department of Agriculture]

Do organic farming methods harm the enviroment?

Organic growers claim that their methods are in harmony with nature and do no damage. But is this entirely true? Supporters of non-organic farming point out that non-organic methods produce a higher yield of crops from the same area of land than organic methods. This leaves more land to grow naturally.

What about nitrates? Many of the natural products used by organic farmers contain large amounts of nitrogen. Even farmyard manure accounts for just under 10 percent of the nitrogen that goes into our soil every year.

Organic farmers use mechanical hoes to pull out weeds instead of chemical weed killers. This shallow hoeing can cause damage to the soil structure and insect life, as well as young birds.

> *Ponds and pollution*

This water is polluted with agricultural chemicals. Nitrates from fertilizer have leached into the pond, allowing mats of algae to grow. The algae block light from the water plants below.

✔ What do they think?

"I'm not worried that non-organic food will hurt me, but there are environmental problems with pesticide use—and health problems for farm workers, especially in poorer, under-regulated countries."

A contributor to an online discussion forum

What is conventional farming doing to the soil?

The soil is the basis of all farming. Without healthy soil, crops will not grow properly. As each plant grows, it takes some nutrients out of the soil. The farmer must replace this, so that the soil always has the right balance of nutrients and other materials. Do artificial fertilizers help to keep that balance?

Deserts and dust storms

Poor quality soils pose an even greater danger to the environment than lack of nutrients. Without the right ingredients binding the soil together, its structure breaks down. It turns to dust, which can easily be washed away by rains or blown away by winds. This is called **erosion**, and it can cause great damage to the environment. Eroded soil builds up in drains, lakes, and rivers and increases the risk of flooding. The polluted water harms wildlife.

Many activities contribute to soil erosion, including the destruction of forests, plowing on hillsides, and over-grazing with livestock. But artificial fertilizers and weed killers share the blame. Nitrates add nothing to the soil structure, while modern weed killers strip away plants that help hold the soil together, leaving a bare surface.

Do organic farming methods protect the soil against erosion? Certainly, the use of organic manures (including animal dung) puts natural materials back into the ground. This helps to make the soil stable and strong, and so less likely to be eroded.

✔ The DDT tragedy

DDT (Dichloro-Diphenyl-Trochloroethane) was one of the earliest modern pesticides. In the 1950s farmers worldwide sprayed it on crops to destroy insect pests. Sadly, the chemical killed beneficial creatures as well, such as bees and butterflies.

Worse still, DDT poisoned animals that ate these insects, including many birds, fish, and rodents. The pesticide was finally banned in most developed countries in the 1980s.

> *Healthy and unhealthy soils*

Soil depletion (creation of poor quality soil) can be caused by overuse for growing crops, too many chemical inputs, such as fertilizers and herbicides, and salinization (excess salt). The quality of soil can make a huge difference to plant growth. Compare the difference in the health of these cress seedlings grown in good and damaged soil.

> *Prairie farming*

Modern farming methods have changed the face of the
landscape so that much more food can be grown.

Can We Change Anything?

On the face of it, we should be happy about our food supply. Never before in history have so many people had enough to eat. In some parts of the developed world, in fact, people have too much to eat. The rate of **obesity** is soaring in the United States and other countries.

This is extraordinary. Less than 100 years ago, millions of people went hungry and millions more suffered from diseases caused by poor diet. In recent decades, these numbers have fallen dramatically. Thanks to modern farming and processing methods, we can produce so much more safe, nourishing food.

But is it all good news? Most of us have enough to eat and can expect to live longer than our grandparents' generation. But is our modern diet making us healthier? Degenerative illnesses, such as cancer, diabetes, and heart disease, are on the rise. Some scientists blame this on the food we eat.

Can this "progress" go on? Today's production levels depend on huge amounts of nitrogen fertilizer. What happens when the oil and other fossil fuels run out? Organic farming claims to offer a partial solution. But can strict organic farming produce enough for a world population that may reach 10 billion by 2050?

Can we change the attitude of farmers?

The job of modern farmers is complicated. They are encouraged to produce as much as possible, not only to make money but also to satisfy the hunger of the growing population. Farming is very demanding work, and many find it hard to survive in business. They have to battle with diseases, bad weather, falling prices, and hundreds of other difficulties. It is no wonder that most of them choose the methods that seem to be the safest and most reliable—chemical fertilizers and pesticides, and intensive animal raising. Why should they change?

Questions to ask

In thinking about the question of whether organic food is better, there are several questions we should ask:

Can organic farmers grow enough?

Some people say organic farming needs more land to grow the same amount of crops as non-organic farming. Others say organic farmers can grow just as much as non-organic. What is the evidence from trials and statistics?

> Challenges for the future
The decisions we take about the way we produce our food will have an important impact on the health of the environment.

Is organic food always going to be more expensive?

Organic food is often more expensive to buy. But is this really because it is more expensive to produce? Will the price come down if more organic food is produced?

What is the real cost of non-organic farming?

Farming with nitrates and other chemicals seems more efficient, but what about the damage and pollution it causes? Who pays to put that right?

Is the present system sustainable?

Eroded topsoil, contamination of water, loss of plant and animal diversity—all these problems are blamed on modern farming methods. How long can it go on? What happens when the chemicals run out?

✔ Why organic?

Why does someone choose to be an organic producer? Here are the words of some organic farmers across the world:

"Treat the Earth well. It was not given to you by your parents. It was loaned to you by your children."

Kenyan proverb

"The most revolutionary act you can commit is to go to a farmers' market and buy from an organic grower. Because then you have bypassed the whole distribution system. You're buying food that's local, so you're supporting your community; you're supporting an agriculture that's benefiting the Earth."

Terence Welch, United States

"You have to give nature an opportunity to participate in the stewardship of the soil. . . We treat the farms as a living organism, while most conventional farmers treat their farms as being sick."

Leontino Balbo, Brazil

"Organic farming delivers the highest quality, best-tasting food, produced without artificial chemicals or genetic modification, and with respect for animal welfare and the environment."

Prince Charles, United Kingdom

"We demonstrated what environment we all need for optimum health and quality of life—clean air, clean pure living water, fertile living soil, and organic, fresh, nutritious food."

Paul Woodhouse, Australia

Organizing your own debate

Is organic food better? Have you made up your mind yet? Having read and thought about the issues of the topic in this book, you should be ready to explain your opinion to other people and persuade them that it is the right one. The best way to do this is to organize a debate with your classmates.

The simplest kind of debate may not be the most effective. You could just start a general discussion with other students, but this can easily turn into a shouting match, and nobody will learn much from it.

✔ The rise of organic food

Worldwide sales of organic food have grown by about 20 percent a year since the 1990s.

✓ In 2002, organic food sales were $23 billion.

✓ In 2006, organic food sales were $40 billion.

Yet these sales are still only about 2 percent of total food sales worldwide.

Two-sided debate

This is a good method for a classroom debate. This formal kind of debate has two sides. One side makes a case for the **motion**. The other side, the opposition, argues against it.

One person is chosen to be the **moderator**, or referee. This person does not take part in the speeches, but directs the debate. He or she introduces the motion and keeps control of the speakers and the audience.

The first speaker on each side makes a speech, giving reasons for his or her opinions. The sides alternate speakers. Each speech should last no longer than five minutes.

The side speaking for the proposition speaks first and last. The final speeches are summaries of the best arguments of each team. There can then be questions from the audience. Lastly, the audience votes on whether or not they agree with the motion. The moderator counts the votes and declares the winner.

> *Discussion with direction*

This is a middle school debate in progress. Well-organized debates allow for a clearer understanding of the issues.

✔ How to be a good debater

✓ Research your subject and prepare your speech thoroughly in advance—this will give you confidence.

✓ Have plenty of facts and other evidence ready.

✓ When speaking, stand up straight and don't move around too much.

✓ Look up and make eye contact with your audience.

✓ Read your speech clearly and loudly enough for everyone to hear, using your natural voice.

✓ Vary the pitch of your voice—this helps to keep the attention of the audience.

✓ Emphasize the key points in your speech.

✓ Speak only when the moderator allows you to.

✓ Listen carefully to what other speakers have to say.

✓ Make a note of the weak points in your opponents' speeches.

Issues to think about

When you started this book, did you have an opinion about organic food? This book has shown you some of the issues involved in both sides of the debate. It should also have helped you learn to think critically, to find and judge evidence, and to make your argument to others effectively.

Here are some of the issues of the subject of organic food that have been raised in this book:

Food for all
Everybody has to eat food to live. Growing food is probably the single most important industry in the world. The way we produce food has changed dramatically in the past 50 years. New chemicals and machines allow farmers to produce more crops than ever before.

What is the difference?
Today, most of our food is produced in a non-organic way, using chemical fertilizers, pesticides, and medicines. None of this is organic. To be organic, farmers must use only natural fertilizers or ground minerals, and pesticides made from natural materials.

Taking care of ourselves
The main aim of farming is to grow enough to feed everyone in the world. Some think farmers can only do this by using large amounts of chemicals. Others believe these chemicals are dangerous to humans in many ways and pose big health risks. They say that organic produce does not contain chemical residues and also tastes better.

Taking care of livestock
We must not forget that farming also affects the lives of many millions of other animals. Huge numbers of pigs, cattle, poultry, and other beasts provide us with food. Most of these farm animals are raised in non-organic and intensive ways. Does this affect their health and the quality of their lives? Organic farmers raise their livestock in more natural conditions. Animals live mainly outdoors and are fed on naturally grown foods. But does this make them any happier?

Taking care of Earth
Food production has a massive effect on the world around us. The future of the planet depends largely on the way we treat the land. So, are non-organic farming methods harming the environment? Are organic methods any better? Organic farmers argue that they are actively caring for the land and trying to grow food in a way that can be sustained for centuries to come.

Being responsible

We should know more about what we eat. But there is more to food and food production than mealtimes. We are also responsible for the future of the environment. How much do we know about the way farming and food processing affects the soil, the water, and the air we breathe?

It is essential to make the link between what we eat and where and how we live. Humans have changed the landscape of Earth so that we can grow food. Are these changes now encouraging environmental disaster? Making this link can be difficult, as we become less connected with where our food comes from and simply get it, wrapped in plastic, from the supermarket. We need to think about the harsh realities of how it was produced. What do you think? Is organic food better?

> **Which one to buy?**

Organic or non-organic? Weigh the
evidence. It's your choice.

Find Out More

Projects

◆ **What's in your food?**
In supermarkets or at home, read the labels on jars and packaging. Do they say the food is organic? Look at the list of ingredients and find out about any you do not recognize.

◆ **Local producers**
Find out about local organic food producers near your home. Look in the telephone directory or on the Internet. Ask stores and restaurants where their food comes from and how it is grown. Try to buy food produced as locally as possible.

◆ **The taste test**
Organize a blind taste test with your friends. Put out a selection of organic and non-organic food side by side—the same varieties of tomatoes, apples, carrots, cheese, and boiled eggs, for example. Then taste each carefully. Can you tell which is organic and which is not? Which tastes better?

◆ **Visit a farm**
Find an organic farm near you and ask if you can visit. You will learn a lot by seeing for yourself how the animals and crops are raised. Next, visit a conventional farm and study the differences.

Books

◆ Bowden, Rob. *Sustainable World: Food and Farming*. San Diego: Kidhaven, 2004. This book explores how food can be grown in a sustainable way.

◆ Farndon, John. *From DNA to GM Wheat: Discovering Genetically Modified Food*. Chicago: Heinemann Library, 2007. This explores the truth about how GM foods came to be developed.

◆ Mason, Paul. *Food: Planet Under Pressure*. Chicago: Heinemann Library, 2006. This studies how climate change is affecting our food supplies.

- Paladino, Catherine. *One Good Apple: Growing Food for the Sake of the Earth*. Boston: Houghton Mifflin, 2000. This book examines the problems of pesticides and the benefits of organic farming.

- Sanger, Rick. *No Eat, Not Food*. Grass Valley, Calif.: Mountain Path, 2006. This is a very entertaining (and award-winning) storybook treatment of organic issues.

Websites

The organic movement

- *www.ifoam.org*
  The wide-ranging site of the International Federation of Organic Agriculture Movements.

- *www.organicconsumers.org*
  The website of the Organic Consumers' Association.

- *www.localharvest.org*
  Local Harvest is a group that promotes organic food and farming and helps consumers find organic food locally.

National and international farming and food

- *www.fao.org*
  The website of the Food and Agriculture Organization, part of the World Health Organization.

- *www.usda.gov*
  The website of the U.S. Department of Agriculture.

Glossary

agroforest	woodland area used for farming
antibiotic	medicine containing substances that destroy organisms causing disease
biased	in favor of one particular view or argument; not open-minded
broiler house	shed used for housing many young chickens that are raised for meat
carbon dioxide	natural gas formed of carbon and oxygen, it is a major factor in global warming
cholesterol	white fatty substance found naturally in plants and animals
concentrate	food in a concentrated (very rich) form
ecosystem	complete environment with its own special organisms living together
erosion	wearing away of rock or soil
fertilizer	material that adds nutrients to the soil and makes it more fertile
flavonoid	substance found in many plants and plant-based foods that fights certain diseases
forage	grass and other natural animal food
fossil fuel	fuel, such as coal, gas, or petroleum, made from the fossilized remains of prehistoric creatures
fungicide	chemical that kills spores, mushrooms, and other fungi
genetic breeding	creation of improved breeds of animal or plant by altering their genetic makeup
growth hormone	natural substance that increases growth

herbicide	chemical that kills plants, particularly unwanted ones
homeopathic	alternative medical treatment based on giving tiny doses of remedies that have similar effects to the disease
intensive farm	farm that raises animals in crowded conditions to increase production and lower costs
livestock	animals raised for meat or some other use
manure	animal dung used to fertilize the soil
microbe	tiny life-form, usually one that causes disease
moderator	person who controls a meeting or assembly
motion	formal proposal or statement that forms the basis of a debate
nitrogen	common element used in the manufacture of artificial fertilizer
nutrient	substance that feeds and nourishes plants or animals
obesity	state of being very overweight
organic	grown with fertilizers and other substances made only of animal or vegetable matter
parasite	organism that lives on or in a plant or animal of another species from which it receives all its nutrition
perennial	something that grows back every year
pesticide	chemical that kills pests of all sorts
protein	chemical compound that plays an important part in animal health, especially the growth and repair of body cells
silage	animal food made by storing fermenting green plants, such as grass
systemic	affecting the entire system of a plant, not just the leaves or stem
vaccine	medicine that prevents serious disease by creating resistance to that disease in the body

Index

agroforestry 15
animal welfare 30–37, 39, 50
antibiotics 12, 19, 35, 37

BSE ("mad cow disease") 33

carbon dioxide emissions 40
chemicals 5, 11, 12, 16, 18, 21, 47, 50
residues in food 24, 25, 50
see also fertilizers; herbicides; pesticides
chicken farming 31, 36, 37
battery chickens 36
broiler houses 36
free range poultry 37
crop spraying 12, 25
annual program 25
organic 25
crop yields 17, 27, 41, 46
cruelty 37

dairy farming 18–19, 31, 32–35
diseases and physical problems 32, 33, 34
high intensity feeding 32–33
medicines 34, 35
milk yields 32, 33, 35
non-organic 18, 32–3, 34
organic 19, 34–5
DDT 42
debates 7, 48–49
debating skills 8, 49
evaluation 48
moderator 48
motion 48
diseases 16, 21, 22, 37, 45
diversity, loss of 47

environmental issues 38–43, 47, 50, 51
non-organic farming 39, 40, 41, 42, 47, 50
organic farming 39, 41, 42, 50

facts 6
famine 17, 26, 27
farmer's markets 7, 47
farming
Green Revolution 17
intensive 12, 31, 36–37, 46
mixed 15
scientific advances 14, 26
traditional 11, 14–15, 16, 37
see also chemicals
fertilizers
chemical 12, 16, 21, 24, 25, 26, 40, 46
natural 14, 18, 50
nitrates 16, 18, 21, 39, 40, 41, 42, 45, 47
flavonoids 22
forest destruction 39, 42
fossil fuels 40, 45
fungicides 25

genetic breeding 26
global warming 40
grain production, falling 27
Green Revolution 17
growth boosters 21, 25, 31, 32

herbicides 16, 24
homeopathic medicines 19, 35

International Federation of Organic Agriculture Movements (IFOAM) 13

livestock farming
intensive 12, 27, 31, 46
organic 31
over-grazing 42
traditional 14, 15

manure 13, 14, 18, 42
medical care
non-organic farming 12, 18, 31, 34, 37
organic farming 19, 34, 35

nitrates 16, 18, 21, 39, 40, 41, 42, 45, 47
in drinking water 21, 40
nitrogen 16, 41
nutrients 13, 26, 42

obesity 45
opinions 6, 7
bias 9
critical judgement 8
evidence for 8, 9
formation 6
organic farming
dairy farming 19, 34–35
definition 12
environmental benefits 39
livestock farming 31
main features 12
opting for 47
principles 13, 50
traditional methods 14–15, 16
organic food
cost 5, 17, 47
definition 12
flavor 28
food sales 48
health benefit claims 22–23
negative argument for 22, 24
nutritional content 26

positive argument for 22–23
reasons for going organic 29
safety issues 21, 23
over-grazing 42

parasites 16
pesticides
chemical 12, 16, 18, 21, 24, 39, 46
DDT 42
"organic" 18, 25, 50
pesticide poisoning 25
residues in food 21, 25
pests 16, 21
pig farming 14, 36
pollution
air 21, 40
water 21, 39, 40, 41, 42, 47
population growth 16, 27

sheep farming 36
soil fertility 15, 42
see also fertilizers
soil structure 41, 42
erosion 42, 47
surplus food 21

U.S. Department of Agriculture 12

vaccines 18

water contamination 21, 39, 40, 41, 42, 47
wheat production 17